T0380643

The book is dedicated for Natalie and Madison.

A

Armadillo

B

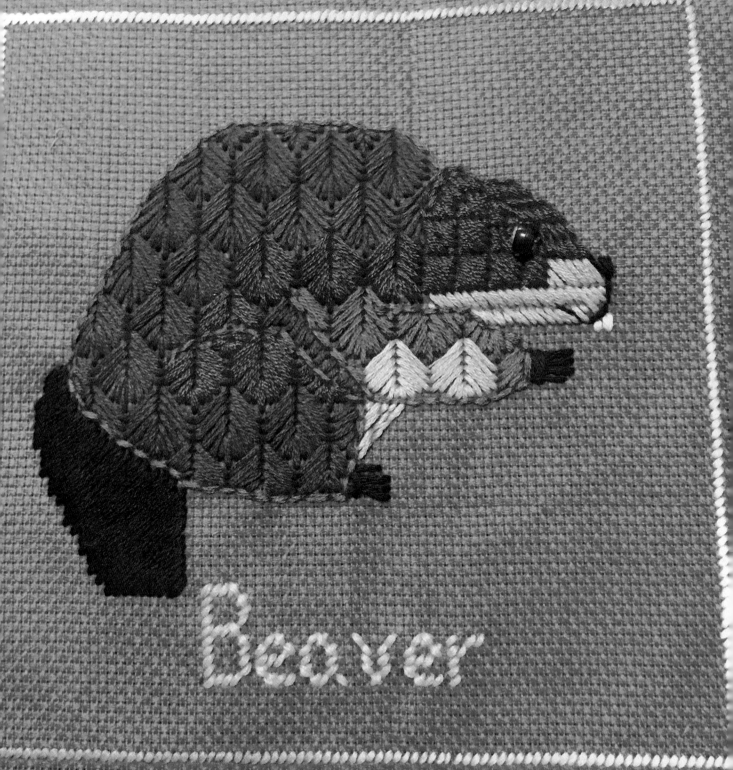

Beaver

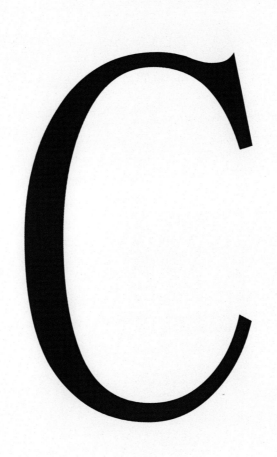

D

Dolphin

E

F

G

Gorilla

H

Hippopotamus

I

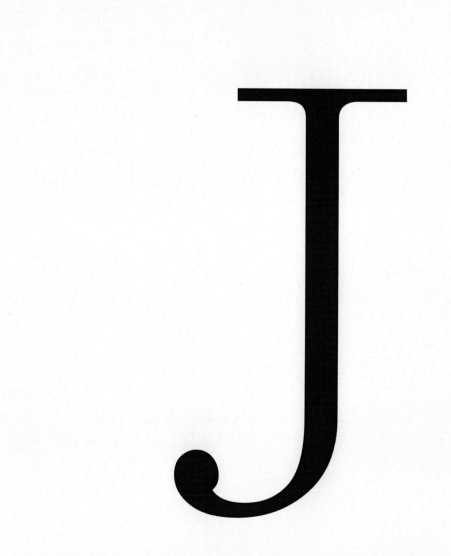

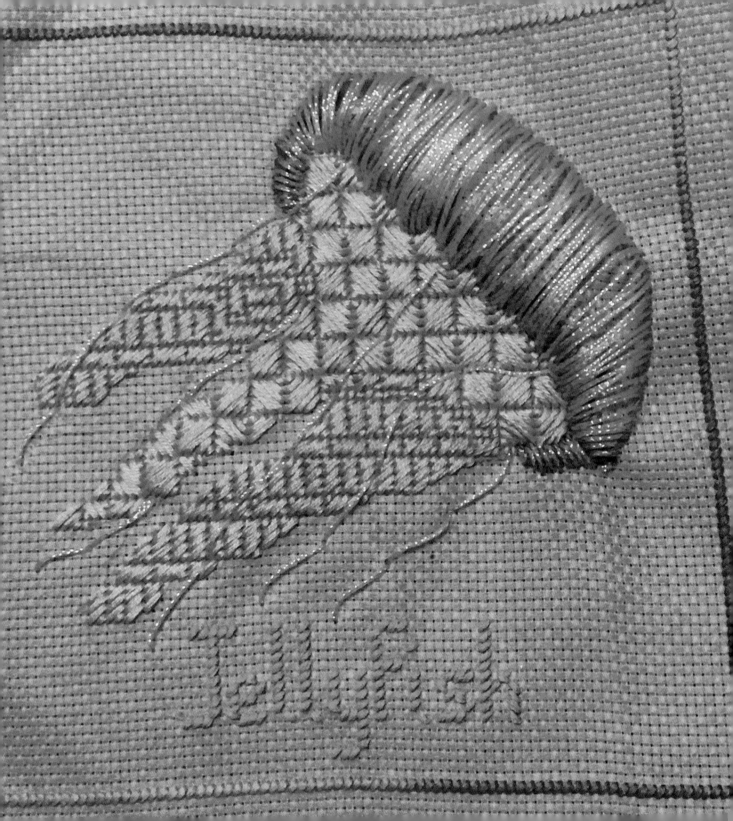

K

Kangaroo

L

M

Moose

N

Octopus

P

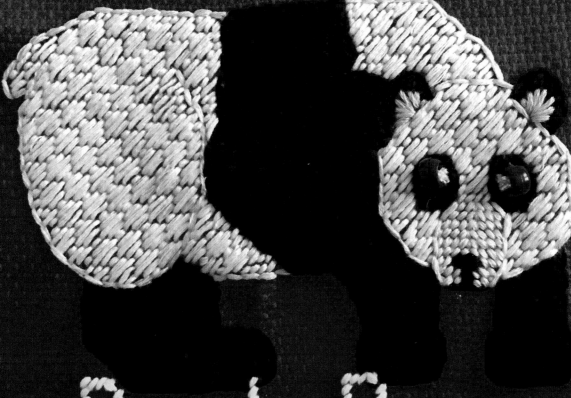

Panda Bear

R

Squirrel

T

Turtle

U

V

W

Walrus

X

X-Ray Fish

Y

Z

Copyright © 2019 by Bethany Brigham. 792216

Library of Congress Control Number: 2019902694

ISBN: Softcover   978-1-7960-1674-1
        Hardcover   978-1-7960-1675-8
        EBook   978-1-7960-1673-4

All rights reserved. No part of this book may
be reproduced or transmitted in any form or by
any means, electronic or mechanical, including
photocopying, recording, or by any information
storage and retrieval system, without permission in
writing from the copyright owner.

The views expressed in this work are solely those of
the author and do not necessarily reflect the views of
the publisher, and the publisher hereby disclaims any
responsibility for them.

Print information available on the last page

Rev. date: 03/06/2019

To order additional copies of this book, contact:
Xlibris
1-888-795-4274
www.Xlibris.com
Orders@Xlibris.com

Printed in the United States
By Bookmasters